Editor Lis Edwards
Designer Neil Smith/Camron
Production Susan Mead

Acknowledgements

Graham Allen/Linden Artists Front cover
Hayward Art Group Back cover, 38–39, 40, 41
Pat Lenander/Temple Art Group 22–23
Vanessa Luff 10–11, 14–15, 26–27, 34–35
David Nash 8
Steve Rigby 12–13, 16–17, 20–21, 24–25,
28–29, 30–31, 32–33, 36–37
Neil Smith 9
George Thompson 18–19
Endpaper photograph M. Thonig/Zefa Picture
Library

Front cover: A common frog sitting on
arrowhead leaves.

Endpapers: A German lake in summer.

Macdonald Educational Ltd
Holywell House
Worship Street
London EC2A 2EN

Printed in Hong Kong

ISBN 0 356 07121 9

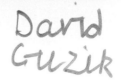

David Guzik

NATURE IN FOCUS

LIFE IN PONDS & STREAMS

Oliver Aston

Macdonald Educational

Contents

All about fresh water

This book is about freshwater life. It looks at different sorts of fresh water, such as ponds and streams, and shows you the plants and animals which live in each one.

What is fresh water?

Nearly three-quarters of the world's surface is covered by water. Most of this water is in the oceans and seas. It tastes salty because of the chemicals dissolved in it. The rest is in rivers, streams, ponds and lakes. This water is called *fresh water* because it is not salty.

Fresh water falls to the earth as rain. Most rain lands in the oceans, but some falls on land. Some sinks into the earth, and eventually seeps into the sea. Some is carried to the sea by rivers.

At the same time, heat from the sun evaporates sea water, drawing it up into the sky where it collects as clouds. The evaporated water is fresh water because the chemicals which taste salty are left behind in the sea. As the clouds cool water droplets form and fall to the earth as rain.

This rise and fall of water is happening all the time. The water rises from the sea, falls as rain, and returns to the sea, and the whole process begins again. We call this a *cycle*.

Water and oxygen

The water cycle is essential for life. All plants and animals need water. Some animals get water by drinking it, others by living in it. Some plants take in water from the earth and some live in water.

Animals also need oxygen. This is easily found on land. The air is full of it, so animals just breathe it in. Vertebrates, like birds and mammals, have lungs. Insects have tiny openings in their skin.

Animals which live in water also need oxygen. The water is full of it. Some is made by plants but most of it is taken in at the surface of the water. Animals have developed special ways of getting oxygen. Some, like fishes and water fleas, can take oxygen from the water. Others, like water beetles and snails, have to go to the surface and take in air.

▲ **A kingfisher sits on its perch, waiting for a fish to move in the water below.**

What is a habitat?

Freshwater animals and plants live in many different places – not just ponds and streams, but also lakes, rivers, canals, reservoirs, ditches – anywhere that water collects. The place where an animal or plant lives is called its *habitat*, its natural surroundings.

Every freshwater habitat is different. In some, like ponds and lakes, the water is still. In others, like streams and rivers, the water is always moving. The temperature of water varies enormously. A mountain stream will be very cold all the year, but a pond will become very warm in summer, and may freeze over in winter. The water may be deep, as in a lake, or shallow, as in a stream.

Different ways of life

Because habitats are all different, each one has different plants and animals. They are adapted to the conditions of the habitat in which they live. For example, pondskaters live on the surface of the water. They skim lightly across it, held up by the surface tension. This means they have to live in still-water habitats, such as ponds. The surface tension is continually broken in the tumbling waters of a fast-flowing stream. But some animals prefer this habitat. The water takes in more oxygen when it is moving fast, so animals which like a lot of oxygen, like trout, live in mountain streams.

The plants and animals in each habitat need each other. Plants are eaten by animals and use their waste matter as food. Animals eat plants or other animals. Plants and animals die or are eaten, and new ones grow or are born. These are just some of the changes that happen all the time, and which affect all the living things in a habitat. This book shows you some of the links between them. You will be able to find many more for yourself.

Looking at ponds

A pond is a shallow hole in the ground which has filled with water. Water plants and insects appear. Frogs come to breed, birds come to nest and drink. Gradually the pond fills with life.

Most ponds were made by people. Some are ornamental, others were dug as drinking-places for cattle or coach-horses. Larger ponds form where chalk and gravel has been dug out.

Every pond is different. One which is overshadowed will have very little life. Rotting leaves make a scum on the surface, keeping oxygen out. Mosquito larvae use tubes to breathe through this, and a few animals feed on the smelly black mud.

A pond in the open gets plenty of sunlight, so that green plants can grow. The water is full of oxygen, so that animals can breathe. Many different plants and animals live there.

▼ How a pond turns into land.

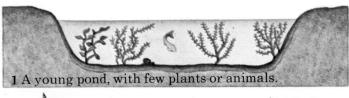

1 A young pond, with few plants or animals.

2 As more plants and animals appear, waste begins to build up on the bottom.

3 The pond is turning into a marsh, as the water gets shallower.

4 The pond has disappeared, leaving a patch of damp earth.

▼ A food pyramid (not to scale). Each arrow means 'eaten by'.

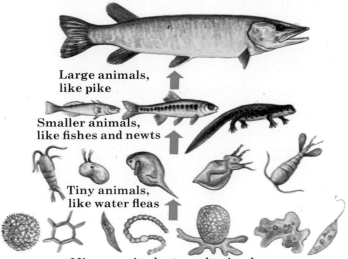

Large animals, like pike

Smaller animals, like fishes and newts

Tiny animals, like water fleas

Microscopic plants and animals

All the plants and animals in a pond eat or are eaten by each other. This can be shown in a diagram, like the **food pyramid** above. The tiniest plants, at the bottom, make food using the energy in sunlight. They are eaten by tiny animals. Larger animals, like small fishes and newts, eat them. They are then eaten by large animals, like the pike at the top.

Another way of showing how energy is passed on is in a **food chain** (below). When the pike dies its body rots, and is used by minute plants and animals to make food.

▼ A food chain (not to scale).

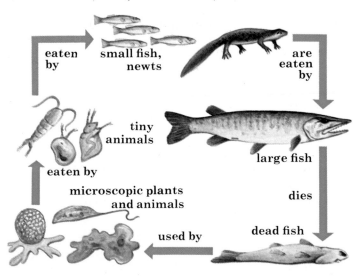

eaten by

small fish, newts

are eaten by

tiny animals

large fish

eaten by

microscopic plants and animals

dies

used by

dead fish

◄ From pond to dry land

Ponds slowly fill in and become dry land. A young pond (**1**) is clear and open. Plants grow in the shallow water at the edge (**2**). As they die their remains form a layer on the bottom. This gets thicker and the water becomes shallower (**3**). Plants grow in the middle of the pond. The pond fills in completely (**4**).

From mountains to the sea

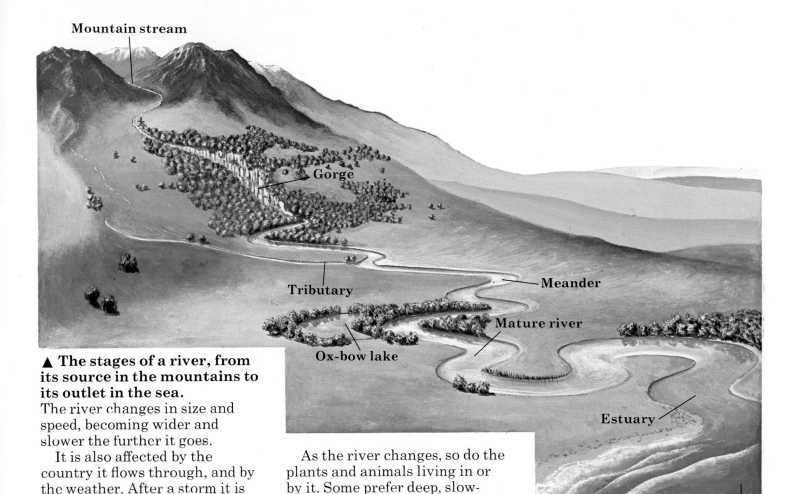

Mountain stream

Gorge

Tributary

Meander

Mature river

Ox-bow lake

Estuary

Sea

▲ **The stages of a river, from its source in the mountains to its outlet in the sea.**
The river changes in size and speed, becoming wider and slower the further it goes.

It is also affected by the country it flows through, and by the weather. After a storm it is deeper and faster, but it may almost dry up in a long hot summer.

As the river changes, so do the plants and animals living in or by it. Some prefer deep, slow-flowing muddy water. Others live in shallow, fast-flowing clear water.

How rivers form

Most rivers start high up in mountains and hills, where the rainfall is heavy, and where there may be melting snow. Some of the water soaks into the ground and some gathers in hollows and between stones, making pools. Some runs over the ground in small channels. These channels join up and a **stream** is formed.

The stream rushes downward, carrying pebbles and gravel. They carve a channel into the soil and soft rock. As the stream moves downhill it is joined by others. Soon the young **river** is a torrent cascading down the hillside.

The river leaves narrow V-shaped valleys as it wears the ground away beneath it. Stones and boulders are swept along, and pile up, making rapids. Soft rock is worn away, leaving deep **gorges** in the hillside.

The ground starts to level out as the river leaves the hills. Large sidestreams, called **tributaries**, join the main stream. The river widens, becomes deeper, and flows more slowly and smoothly.

The valley sides are now gentle slopes. The **mature river** flows too slowly to carry boulders, but mud and sand are still swept along.

As the land becomes flatter the river starts to curve from side to side. It forms large loops, called **meanders**. On the outside curve of each meander the river flows fast, eating away the bank and making the loop larger. On the inside curve it flows slowly. Sediment (mud and sand) which has been eroded (cut away) from the banks is dropped here. Eventually the meander will be cut off from the river and form an **ox-bow lake**.

The river has become wide and slow-flowing by the time it reaches the sea. It is carrying huge amounts of soil, which has been eroded from the banks. Much of this is dropped in the **estuary**, where it forms mudflats and sandbanks.

A mountain stream

▲ River crayfish

The crayfish is a large crustacean, up to 6cm long.

During the day the crayfish hides under stones or in a burrow in the bank. At night it crawls over the bottom, feeding on snails, and insect larvae. It only lives in clean water.

▲ An adult **salmon** (9) rising to take a mayfly. It has returned from the sea to the stream where it was hatched.

No one knows how salmon find their way back to their native streams. They may remember the smell of the water, or use the sun's position.

▲ On the stony bed of the stream a **stone loach** (19) is looking for food. It eats stonefly and mayfly nymphs, and usually hunts at night.

Perched on a nearby rock is a male **ring ouzel** (11), looking for insects. It has a clear fluting call, and is a summer visitor. In winter it flies as far south as Africa.

On the other side of the stream is a patch of boggy ground, where **cotton grass** (3) grows. In late spring its seedheads burst, so that it looks like cotton wool, and the fluffy white seeds are blown away.

Key		
1 Rushes	**9** Salmon	**18** Caddis-fly larva
2 Hawthorn	**10** Mayfly	**19** Stone loach
3 Cotton grass	**11** Ring ouzel	**20** Liverworts
4 White willow	**12** Freshwater shrimp	**21** Water moss
5 Heather	**13** Miller's thumb	**22** Brown trout
6 Bracken	**14** Crayfish	**23** Grey wagtail
7 Royal fern	**15** Minnow	**24** Eel
8 Hart's-tongue fern	**16** Mayfly nymph	**25** Horse leech
	17 Stonefly nymph	**26** Dipper

High in the mountains streams rush down rocky slopes, into rock pools and over shallow rapids. The current is too fast for many plants to take root on the stony bed, and few tiny animals can live here.

The water is cold, but clear and full of dissolved oxygen. The animals and plants here prefer these conditions.

▼ **Bracken** (6) and **heather** (5) cover the mountainside. Bracken can grow up to 2.5 metres high, and gives shelter to many small animals, such as rabbits.

Heather is a tough, low plant. In late summer it has purple flowers, loved by bees.

In the damp soil near the water grow **hart's-tongue fern** (8) and **royal fern** (7). Ferns have no flowers. They spread by spores, which grow on the underside of the leaves in autumn. When ripe the spores blow away.

▼ **Buffalo gnat and pupa**
Swarms of these tiny black biting flies gather near water in the summer. Their larvae live in running water, attached to stones.

Each larva turns into a pupa, and spins a silken cocoon fastened to a stone, and filled with air. When the adult fly is ready to emerge it floats to the surface in a bubble of air and flies away.

▲ The long green fronds of **water moss** (21) trail in the fast-flowing water. Its Latin name is *Fontinalis antipyretica*. The second word means 'against fire', because it burns very badly.

The **brown trout** (22) likes fast-flowing, cold water, which contains a lot of oxygen. It is well camouflaged by its spots.

▲ A **dipper** (26) walks underwater. It can swim and dive well, and finds its food among the stones on the stream-bed.

Above it a **grey wagtail** (23) is perched on a rock. This is a male (cock) bird, which has a black summer bib. The wagtail eats insects, which it snatches as they fly above the water.

▼ **Horse leech**
A horse leech eating a river snail. It also eats worms and larvae, which it swallows whole.

Leeches are very common in fresh water. They vary from 1cm to 15cm long.

Water-birds

Male

Female

Freshwater habitats are full of birds. They come to drink, to bathe, and to feed on the great variety of plants and animals there.

Some, like mallard, live on the water. They have developed webbed feet to help them swim. Others, like herons, live on land but visit water to feed.

*Not to scale. The size given is the body-length of a mature adult.

▲ **Pied wagtail** 18cm
A perky bird, often seen by rivers wagging its long tail, or running along the bank. It eats small insects such as flies, beetles and moths, which it catches on the wing.

▲ **Grey wagtail** 18cm
One of the most colourful wagtails, seen near fast-flowing water. It eats mostly insects, such as flies, nymphs and small beetles. The male (left) has a black bib in summer.

▲ **Kingfisher** 16.5cm
Usually seen as a flash of blue darting along a stream or river. It dives from a perch and spears small fishes, which it swallows head first so that the scales lie flat.

▲ **Reed warbler** 12.5cm
Lives in reed-beds, where it eats flies and moths, and berries in autumn. Its cup-shaped nest is woven round reed stems. In winter it flies south, sometimes as far as Africa.

▲ **Heron** 90cm
A tall, silent, wading bird seen by rivers, lake and ponds. It stands on one leg or stalks small animals, such as frogs, fishes and water-voles. It has a slow, flapping flight and nests in colonies in trees.

Waterbirds in flight

You can identify birds by the way they fly, and the shape of their bodies.

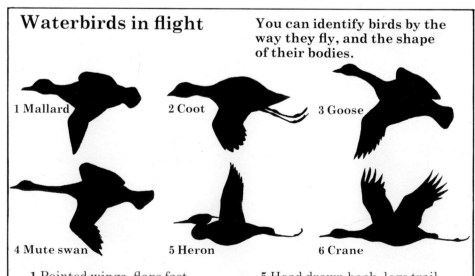

1 Mallard
2 Coot
3 Goose
4 Mute swan
5 Heron
6 Crane

1 Pointed wings, flaps fast.
2 Round wings, legs trail, weak flier. 3 Long neck, often in flocks. 4 Long neck, slow flight.

5 Head drawn back, legs trail, slow flight. 6 Neck outstretched, legs trail, slow flight.

▲ **Dipper** 18cm
A chunky little bird, seen
perched on rocks or flying low
and fast along mountain streams.
Its brown and white plumage
hide it well among the brown
rocks and white water.

It catches insects, tadpoles and
small fishes underwater.

▲ **Snipe** 37cm
A striped bird, often seen in
marshy ground, using its long
bill to probe for worms, snails
and insect larvae. When
disturbed it flies up with a harsh
call. In the breeding season the
tail feathers of the male make a
bleating sound in flight.

▲ **Water rail** 28cm
Seen at dusk and dawn, hunting
in reed-beds for tiny animals
such as spiders, freshwater
shrimps and worms. It darts from
cover to cover with a high-
stepping walk or flies for a few
seconds. You may hear its high
sharp cry in the evening.

Male

Chicks

▲ **Mallard** 58cm
A common duck, seen swimming
on ponds, lakes and rivers or
flying overhead. It 'up-ends' or
dabbles in the water to find food,
mainly plants. The male (bottom)
is called a drake, and is brightly
coloured.

▲ **Coot** 38cm
A large bird, often seen
swimming on lakes or slow-
flowing rivers, or grazing on the
banks. It eats plants and small
water animals, such as tadpoles.
When disturbed it gives a loud,
high-pitched cry.

▲ **Moorhen** 35cm
A large bird, seen swimming or
diving near the banks of lakes,
ponds and slow-flowing rivers. It
eats seeds, water plants, worms,
snails and insect larvae. When
alarmed it can sink, leaving only
its bill above water.

A river

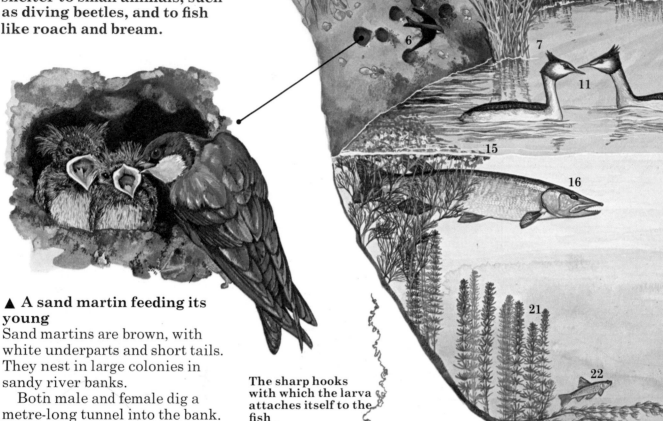

As the river flows downwards the ground becomes flatter. Trees and bushes grow on the banks, some planted there to stop the soil crumbling away.

The water flows more slowly, is warmer and cloudy. Water plants can take root on the muddy bottom. They give shelter to small animals, such as **diving beetles**, and to fish like **roach** and **bream**.

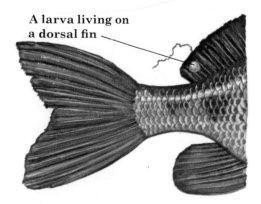

▲ A sand martin feeding its young

Sand martins are brown, with white underparts and short tails. They nest in large colonies in sandy river banks.

Both male and female dig a metre-long tunnel into the bank. Then they hollow out a chamber and line it to make the nest. The young birds are fed on insects which the parents catch as they fly over the water.

The sharp hooks with which the larva attaches itself to the fish

A larva living on a dorsal fin

◀ ▲ Swan mussel larva

Swan mussels live on the muddy beds of ponds, lakes and rivers, and are up to 20cm long.

After laying her eggs, the female keeps them in her gills until spring. The larvae then swim out and hook on to a passing fish. They live on the fish for 2 to 3 weeks and then fall to the bottom, where they develop into mussels.

▲ A **pike** (16) swims fast after the **roach**. It has been hiding in the water plants, camouflaged by its patterned skin. Nothing can escape from its backward-sloping upper teeth.

Swimming above are two **great crested grebes** (11). They are in their summer plumage, with ruffs and ear-tufts. These are used in the courtship display which these birds perform.

14

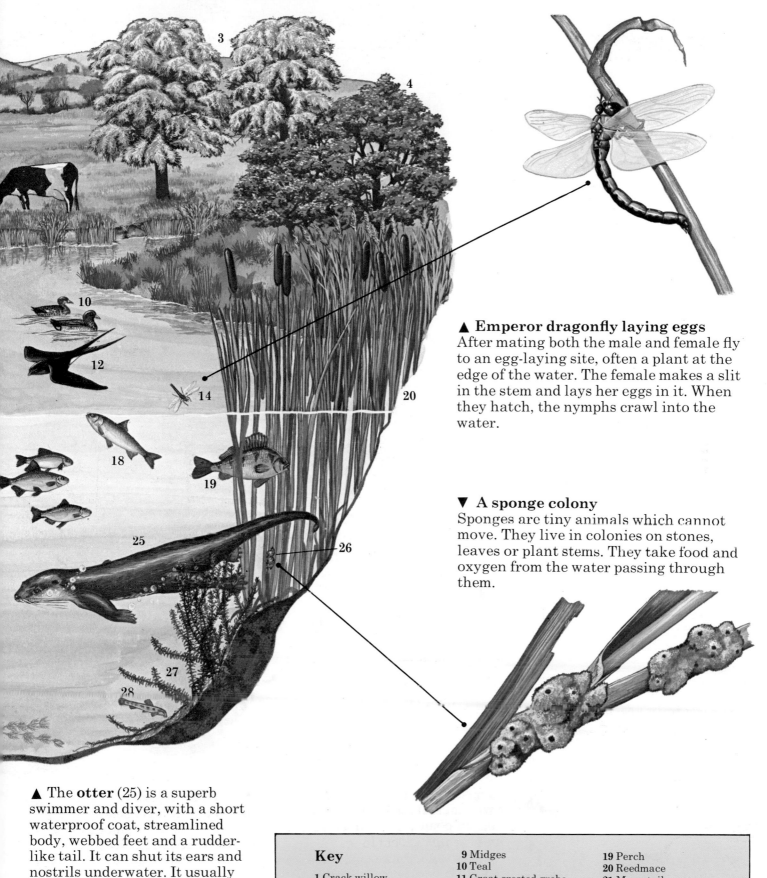

▲ Emperor dragonfly laying eggs
After mating both the male and female fly to an egg-laying site, often a plant at the edge of the water. The female makes a slit in the stem and lays her eggs in it. When they hatch, the nymphs crawl into the water.

▼ A sponge colony
Sponges are tiny animals which cannot move. They live in colonies on stones, leaves or plant stems. They take food and oxygen from the water passing through them.

▲ The **otter** (25) is a superb swimmer and diver, with a short waterproof coat, streamlined body, webbed feet and a rudder-like tail. It can shut its ears and nostrils underwater. It usually hunts at night, and is very shy.

Skimming over the water is a **swallow** (12). Its tiny beak opens very wide to snatch insects, and its curved wings help it to change direction quickly.

Key		
	9 Midges	19 Perch
	10 Teal	20 Reedmace
1 Crack willow	11 Great crested grebe	21 Marestail
2 Swifts	12 Swallow	22 Gudgeon
3 White willow	13 Mayfly	23 Shrew
4 Alder	14 Emperor dragonfly	24 Spiked water milfoil
5 Mute swan	15 Water crowfoot	25 Otter
6 Sand martin	16 Pike	26 Sponge
7 Bulrush	17 Roach	27 Canadian pondweed
8 Stonefly	18 Dace	28 Stone loach

Fishes

The fishes living in fresh waters can be as tiny as minnows or as large as pike. Some, like trout, prefer clear, cold, fast-running mountain streams. Others, like bream, prefer muddy, warm, slow-flowing lowland rivers or lakes.

*Not to scale. The size given is the body-length of a mature adult.

Male in breeding colours

▲ **Gudgeon** 10–15cm
A small fish, varying from grey-green to blackish-grey. Usually found in shallow water over gravel. It swims in small shoals close to the bottom and uses its feeler-like barbels to find food. It eats mostly insect larvae, shrimps and plants.

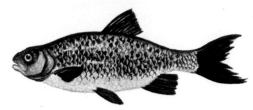

▲ **Chub** 35–50cm
Lives in clear rivers and streams, and varies in colour from dark green to greyish blue. The young live in shoals, but the adult fish is solitary, living in deep water near river banks. It eats mainly small fishes, crayfish, insects and plants.

▲ **Minnow** 5–7cm
A tiny fish, often seen in large shoals of up to 100 fishes near the surface of shallow water. It eats insect larvae, tiny crustaceans and algae. In winter it lives in deeper water.

In summer the male changes to his breeding colours: green sides with black bars, scarlet belly and bronze-green head.

▲ **Grayling** 30–45cm
A slim fish, which you can recognize by its long dorsal fin. It lives in fast-flowing rivers and mountain lakes, often in small shoals. Most of the animals it eats live on the bottom, such as insect larvae, snails and freshwater shrimps.

▲ **Barbel** 75-90cm
A large fish which lives in clear, fairly fast-flowing rivers with gravel bottoms. At night it hunts for food on the bottom, using its barbels to find worms, molluscs and insect larvae. During the day it rests in deep water near the bank.

▲ **Perch** 20–35cm
You can recognise this fish by the dark bars on its sides. The perch lives in deep water in rivers and lakes, often among weeds. It eats crustaceans, such as freshwater shrimps, the larvae of insects such as water beetles, and small fishes.

▲ **Pike** 40–100cm
A large fish, found in rivers and lakes. It is usually greenish, with gold spots and bars on its sides. This pattern helps to hide the pike as it waits among water plants for smaller fishes. It is a fierce hunter and sometimes eats water voles or ducklings.

▲ **Roach** 15–30cm
A medium-sized fish which lives in slow-flowing rivers and lakes. The young eat small crustaceans, such as freshwater shrimps. The adults eat mainly plants, with some insect larvae and snails. In colder weather roach often stop feeding.

▲ **Silver bream** 15cm
A rounded, humpbacked fish which lives in weedbeds near the bottom of rivers and deep lakes. It feeds on insect larvae and molluscs.

During the breeding season shoals gather in shallow water. The fish are very active and will leap out of the water and splash at the surface.

▲ **Brown trout** 18–35cm
Brown trout live in cold, fast-flowing water, usually in mountain rivers and lakes. They eat insects, insect larvae, crustaceans and smaller fishes. River trout have red spots and greenish-brown sides. Lake trout are usually smaller than river trout, and are often silver with black spots.

▲ **Dace** 20–25cm
Lives in fairly fast-flowing rivers and streams, and in some lakes. It prefers clean, shallow water and is often found in large shoals near the surface.

The dace eats snails, insects, freshwater shrimps and plants. It moves into shallow water over gravel or stones to spawn.

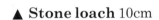

▲ **Miller's thumb** 10cm
A small fish, also called a bullhead, with a flattened head. Its colour varies from dark grey to brown.

It is usually found in fast-flowing water, hiding under stones during the day. At night it hunts slow-moving animals such as insect larvae, which it swallows whole.

▲ **Stone loach** 10cm
A small, rounded fish whose back varies in colour from dark olive to blue. It lives in rivers, streams and ponds.

The stone loach hides in a hollow under stones on the bottom during the day. At night it hunts insect larvae and crustaceans, which it finds on the bottom.

▲ **Common bream** 30–40cm
A dull bronze or grey fish which looks like the silver bream but is more common. It lives in large slow-moving rivers, lakes and reservoirs.

At night it feeds in the mud on the bottom. It eats small animals such as worms, insects, insect larvae and molluscs.

The parts of a fish

All fishes have the same parts, though they may look different. For instance, part of the dorsal fin of a stickleback is split into spines.

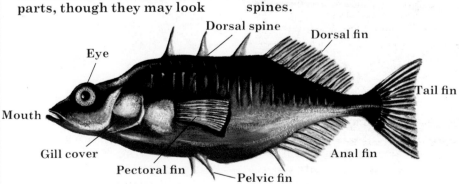

This male stickleback is in his bright breeding colours. For the rest of the year his back is greenish-black and his underparts are silvery. This helps to hide him against the dark stream bed below and the light sky above.

▲ **Eel** Male 30–50cm, female 90–150cm
Eels hatch as leaf-shaped larvae near the Sargasso Sea. Currents carry them to European coastal waters, where they change into elvers, about 10 cm long. These swim up into rivers and streams, where they become adults. They eat almost anything.

Spring

The yearly cycle
Plants need light and warmth. This means that they grow most quickly in summer, when the days are long and warm. Winter days are short and cold, and most plants die down.

Animals need food and warmth. They eat plants, so they too are most active in summer. This is when many animals have their young because there is plenty of food for them.

▲ **Sallow flowers in early spring. The male catkins (left) are yellow with pollen, which is blown on to the green female catkins (right).**

Life begins again
In spring the days become longer and warmer. Plants and animals become active after the cold, dark winter. Animals wake up from their winter rest and look for mates, plants grow new leaves, seeds and bulbs sprout.

Along the riverbank catkins appear on bare willow twigs. Each is a collection of tiny flowers. Pollen from the male catkins is blown on to the female catkins. Because there are no leaves, more of the pollen may reach them. Sallow is often called pussy willow, because its male catkins are silver-grey and fluffy.

▲ **Marsh marigolds flower in early spring. They grow in damp soil and have large shiny yellow flowers. These attract the few insects about.**

Birds look for mates. The males of many species have brightly-coloured feathers to attract females. The mallard drake, with his dark green head and white collar, is often seen.

Great crested grebes grow ruffs and ear-tufts, and perform their mating display. They 'dance' and give each other water-weeds, which they use to build a nest.

Underwater
Water animals become active as the water warms up. This is the breeding season for fishes, and many of them change colour.

The male stickleback's throat and belly become scarlet, his back light green and his eyes bright blue. He builds a nest in which the female lays her eggs.

▲ **Toads lay their eggs in long strings of spawn (top) which wind round water plants. Frogs lay eggs in masses of jelly (bottom).**

Frogs mate and lay great masses of eggs in jelly. After they have been laid the jelly swells and the eggs rise to the surface, where they float.

Water shrews scurry about, thin after the winter. They shed their thick winter coat and grow a short summer one.

Insects in spring
Some insects live through the winter. Water scorpions rest under stones on the bank. Others spend the winter as pupae. One of the earliest butterflies to emerge is the pale yellow brimstone, often seen on a sunny day late in winter.

▲ **The moorhen builds an untidy nest of reeds and sticks in plants near the water. The female lays five to eleven purplish eggs.**

Mayflies live through the winter as nymphs, moving sluggishly in the mud at the bottom of ponds and streams. Fully grown nymphs turn into adults in late spring. They float to the surface and shed a first skin. Many are eaten by fishes.

The ones which escape fly to nearby plants and cling to their stems. After a few hours they cast off another skin and fly off as adult mayflies.

If they are not snapped up by birds or leaping fish they may live for a few hours or even days.

By the end of spring there are insects everywhere, a source of food for many larger animals.

Summer

As summer approaches the days get longer and warmer. Summer is the busiest time of the year for plants and animals. There is plenty of time to find food, and it is easy to keep warm.

The bank is thick with plants and bright with their flowers: pink Himalayan balsam and willowherb, pale blue speedwell and forget-me-not. Many summer flowers are pink or blue, while spring flowers are often yellow.

▲ Sallow leaves appear after the catkins. They are broad and oval, greyish-green with silvery undersides. Other willows have narrow leaves.

Insect life

Most flowering plants are pollinated by insects, which are attracted by the sweet scent and bright colours of the flowers. As the insects suck nectar, pollen grains are caught in the hairs on their legs and bodies. When they settle on another flower the pollen may be rubbed off and fertilize the flower.

Butterflies sun themselves on flowers. Their eggs are hatching into greedy caterpillars, which munch the leaves of plants all day long. They will do this for many weeks, shedding a skin every time it gets too tight, until they are ready to pupate.

▲ Dragonflies rest with their wings spread out on each side of them. Damselflies rest with their wings together over their backs.

Each caterpillar will then stop eating and grow a hard covering. It is now called a pupa. The pupa changes slowly into an adult butterfly. This takes a long time, and many butterflies spend the winter as pupae.

Dragonflies flash across the water like jewels. They are among the fastest flying insects in the world, and are thought to reach speeds of 40kph.

Birds and chicks

The air is full of humming, droning insects, snapped up by hungry swallows, swifts and sand martins. Their eggs have hatched, and their hungry chicks demand food from morning to night. The parent birds spend all day on the wing catching food.

▲ The frogs and toads hatched this spring will not be ready to breed for three years. These are a mature toad (top) and frog (bottom).

Some birds are summer visitors, such as sand martins, sedge warblers and swallows. Their chicks grow fast, and by the end of summer are ready to fly south with their parents.

Waterbirds are also busy feeding their fluffy chicks. Some eggs are eaten by animals like foxes, and many chicks will be eaten by pike and herons. This helps to keep a balance between animals.

In the water

The eggs laid in spring by frogs, toads and newts are hatching. Many have been eaten, but there are still thousands left.

▲ A female moorhen with her chicks, pecking for tiny insects and seeds on the bank. They will run to the water if there is any danger nearby.

Later in summer tadpoles and newt larvae will grow legs and lungs and lose their tails, ready to move on to dry land. Many of them will be eaten then, snatched up by birds as they leave the water.

By late summer seedheads are developing on plants. Many small animals die after breeding, and their places have been taken by their young, born in early summer.

Summer has been a peak time. Plenty of food, warmth and light have made living easy. Both animals and plants have made new growth and built up stores for the coming winter.

Water plants

Plants grow in water in several different ways. Some, like water-lilies, grow in deep water, rooted in the mud. The roots of floating plants, like duckweed, hang free.

Plants like arrowhead are rooted near the water's edge. Right at the edge grow tall plants.

*Not to scale. The height of upright plants is given.

All flowering plants have the same parts, whether they grow on land or in water.

Some do not have all of these parts. For example, marsh marigold flowers have no petals.

The parts of a plant

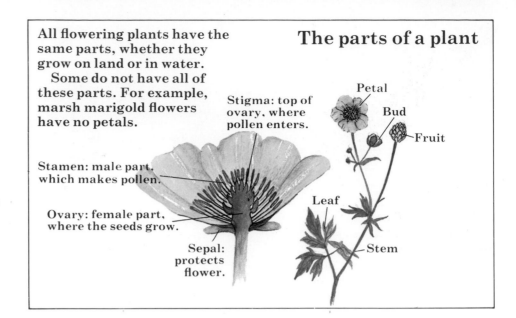

Stigma: top of ovary, where pollen enters.

Petal

Bud

Fruit

Stamen: male part, which makes pollen.

Ovary: female part, where the seeds grow.

Leaf

Sepal: protects flower.

Stem

▲ **Water dropwort** 60cm
A member of the parsley family, with a smooth, hollow stem and fern-like leaves. It grows in ditches and shallow ponds. In summer it has large branched heads of tiny pinkish-white flowers.

▲ **Water plantain** 100cm
A tall, upright plant rooted in the mud at the edge of ponds, ditches and streams.

The broad leaves are held out of the water on long stalks. The three-petalled white flowers only open in the afternoon.

▲ **Arrowhead** 100cm
The name comes from the shape of the upper leaves. The lower ones are ribbon-like, and trail underwater. The male flowers are white with a purple centre, but the female flowers have no petals.

▲ **Watercress** 15-60cm
A wild herb, which grows in shallow water. Clusters of four-petalled white flowers are followed by long thin green seedpods. It is the same as the plant which we eat in salads, but should not be eaten.

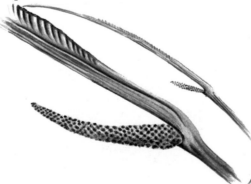

▲ **Sweet flag** 100cm
A tall plant, found by ponds, canals and rivers. Sometimes it grows a tight spike of tiny flowers. Its leaves smell of tangerines when crushed. In medieval times they were used to scent rooms.

▲ **Bistort**
Another name for this plant is snakeweed. When it grows in water it has smooth floating leaves (shown here). On land it has hairy leaves. Both forms have clusters of reddish-white flowers.

▲ Marestail 75cm
The unbranched, erect stems can be seen in ponds and slow-moving water. The stiff thin leaves grow in whorls round the stem. In summer tiny green flowers appear where the leaves join the stem.

▲ Water crowfoot
Grows in ponds, streams and shallow rivers. The underwater leaves are fern-like, but the floating ones are glossy and like clover leaves. It is a member of the buttercup family, and has white buttercup-like flowers.

▲ Spiked water milfoil
The long, flexible stems grow underwater, rooted in the mud in ponds and shallow streams. The flowers appear above water, with the red male flowers higher than the female ones. It is pollinated by the wind.

▲ Broad-leaved pondweed
Found in most fresh waters. The floating leaves are large and oval but the submerged ones are long and thin. The tiny, greenish flowers have no petals. They grow clustered on tall spikes above the water.

▲ Frogbit
A floating plant, which has kidney-shaped leaves and white flowers above water. In autumn it grows shoots which then sink to the bottom. In spring they rise to the surface and grow into new plants.

▲ White water-lily
A beautiful plant, which grows rooted in the mud at the bottom of rivers, lakes and ponds. The leaves and flowers float on the surface during the day. At night the flowers close and sink below the water.

▲ Canadian pondweed
Grows in still water and spreads very fast. The purplish flowers float on the surface but the stem and leaves are underwater. In winter buds grow on the roots and stems. They drop off and grow into new plants.

▲ Hornwort
This is a free-floating plant which grows completely underwater. Pollen is carried from male flowers to female flowers by water. It has stiff, finely-divided leaves and is found in still water.

▲ Duckweed
The green covering on many ponds and ditches is made up of thousands of tiny plants. Each one is a single leaf-like disc with a root. It spreads by growing buds, which break off and form new plants.

Day and night

Many different animals live beside or in water. Some are active during the day and rest at night (left). Others are *nocturnal*: they are active at night (right).

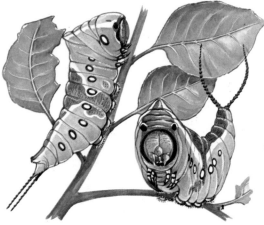

▲ **Puss moth caterpillars**
The puss moth caterpillar feeds mainly on poplar and willow leaves. It is large and brightly coloured. If threatened by an attacker, such as a bird, it rears up and displays its red markings. It also squirts acid.

▲ **Marsh fritillary**
The marsh fritillary is a small butterfly, found in colonies near marshy ground and in damp meadows. It has a weak, fluttering flight and often rests with its wings open. The caterpillar eats scabious leaves.

▲ It is late afternoon. Small mammals are active, like the **water vole**, **stoat** and **grey squirrel**. In the water a **brown rat** hunts tadpoles and insects. Fish swim near the surface, warmed by the sun. A **heron** hunts them from the bank.

Insects fly everywhere in the sunshine. They feed on the open flowers of the **yellow water-lily** and pollinate them.

A **water bat** flits low over the water, catching insects. This bat is seen in daylight. It leaves its roost before sunset.

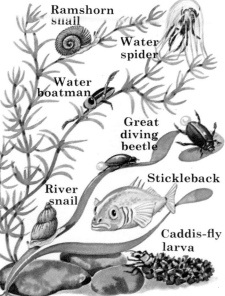

▲ Puss moth

These large, night-flying moths feed on willows, poplars and aspens. They get their name from their thick, furry bodies, which suggest a cat. The female puss moth is larger than the male.

◄ More **bats** fly at night. They use their acute hearing to find flying insects such as moths and beetles.

A **fox** has come to the water to drink and catch small animals such as frogs and water voles. It also takes eggs and chicks from nests.

▼ At night most **water animals** rest. They do not sleep, but stop moving and shelter in water plants. Without light the temperature of the water falls and plants stop making food.

Ramshorn snail
Water spider
Water boatman
Great diving beetle
River snail
Stickleback
Caddis-fly larva

▲ Night has fallen. In the river, life is slower. Most water animals rest on or near the bottom, but a few, like the **eel** and the **crayfish**, are more active at night.

Larger animals hunt at night, hidden by the darkness. The **otter** rests in its holt during the day. You may see an otter playing in the water at night if you are lucky.

Above it is a **tawny owl**, which has caught a vole. Owls sleep during the day and hunt at night. They fly silently on downy wings.

Insects and other tiny animals

Animals without backbones are called invertebrates. They are all quite small, and many have a hard covering. Insects are one large group of invertebrates.

Many invertebrates live near water. Some, like slugs, have to keep moist. Others, like dragonflies, spend the first part of their lives in water.

Since they are small, invertebrates are often eaten by other animals.

*Not to scale. The size given is the body-length of a mature adult.

▲ **Common damselfly** 35mm, wingspan 45mm
Found flying near still and slow-flowing water during the summer. Its green or brown nymphs live underwater for about two years. Nymphs and adults both eat smaller insects.

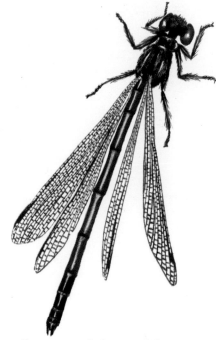

▲ **Large red damselfly** 35mm, wingspan 45mm
Like all damselflies, the common red rests with its wings folded together above its back. It is seen flying over lakes and slow-flowing rivers. The nymphs are short and dark brown.

▲ **Golden-ringed dragonfly** 70mm, wingspan 95mm
A large, powerful flier which hunts insects over fast-flowing rivers and streams during the summer, and can be seen after dark. Its nymph is dark brown and hairy, and hides in mud.

▲ **Common aeshna** 70mm, wingspan 95mm
A long slim dragonfly, common near water in mountain and moorland areas. This is a male, with blue eyes and body. The females and young males are usually green or yellow.

▲ **Broad-bodied libellula** 45mm, wingspan 70mm
A darter dragonfly, which makes short flights from a perch. It has a broad, flat body. The male is blue, and the female is brown. It flies near still or slow-moving water.

The life cycle of a dragonfly

1 The nymph climbs a plant stem.

2 Its skin cracks and the adult emerges.

3 The dragonfly's wings expand.

Dragonfly eggs hatch into nymphs, without wings. The nymph lives underwater for up to four years. Then it climbs out of the water.

The nymph's skin bursts and an adult dragonfly emerges. Its wings expand and stiffen, then it flies off. It will live for about a month.

▲ **Great grey slug** 15cm
This common slug lives in damp places and is active at night or in wet weather. It eats plants or dead animals, and can 'smell' food with its tentacles. It lays eggs which hatch into tiny slugs.

▲ **Common gnat** 7mm
This is a mosquito, often seen near stagnant water. It lays its eggs in raft-like batches on the water surface. The larvae and pupae both hang head downwards from the surface, breathing through tubes.

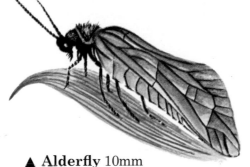

▲ **Alderfly** 10mm
Usually seen resting in large numbers on waterside plants in early summer. It sits with its wings folded like a roof. The larvae live underwater for up to two years, but the adults only live for about three weeks.

▲ **Drone-fly** 15–19mm
A common hover-fly, which looks like a honey-bee but does not sting. It flies in a series of quick darts. The larva, which lives in water, is called a rat-tailed maggot, because of its long breathing tube.

▲ **Common grasshopper** 25mm
Found in grassy places, especially during the summer, when the male chirps. It eats mainly grass. In autumn the female lays eggs in pods. The nymphs hatch in spring, looking like tiny wingless adults.

Larva

▲ **Reed beetle** 8mm
Also called a 'living jewel' because of its shiny colour. The larvae live underwater and breathe air trapped in reed stems. The adults can be seen in summer, running over water plants or flying.

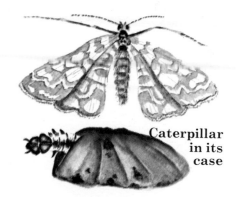

Caterpillar in its case

▲ **China mark moth** 15mm
Seen after dark near stagnant or slow-flowing water. It lays eggs under the leaves of floating plants. The caterpillar makes a floating shelter from oval pieces of leaf, and feeds on the leaves of water plants.

A river bank

The bank is the place where land and water meet, and is full of life.

The soil is soft and damp, ideal for many different plants. Voles and mink tunnel into the soft soil to make their burrows.

Many birds find their food in the water, but nest on the bank.

▶ **Trees** which grow near water are often pollinated by the wind and have catkins to help spread their pollen.

Aspens (1) have thick yellow male catkins and green female ones. In early summer the female catkins turn white and fluffy.

▼ Alder

This tree is often planted to protect banks from being washed away, because its long roots help to bind the soil together. In spring it has catkins. By autumn these have become brown cones, which contain seeds.

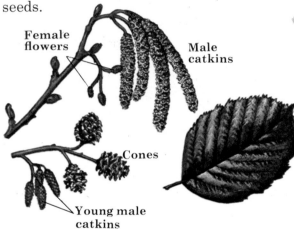

Female flowers

Male catkins

Cones

Young male catkins

▶ A **grey heron** (22) stands in the reeds waiting to spot a fish or frog. It will stand like this for a long time, so one leg is tucked up to keep it warm.

When it sees a fish, the heron will spear it and swallow it whole.

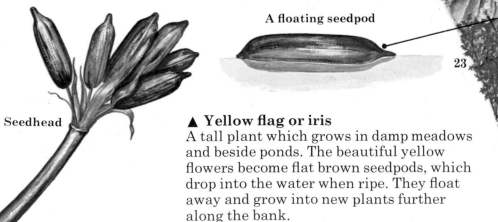

A floating seedpod

Seedhead

▲ Yellow flag or iris

A tall plant which grows in damp meadows and beside ponds. The beautiful yellow flowers become flat brown seedpods, which drop into the water when ripe. They float away and grow into new plants further along the bank.

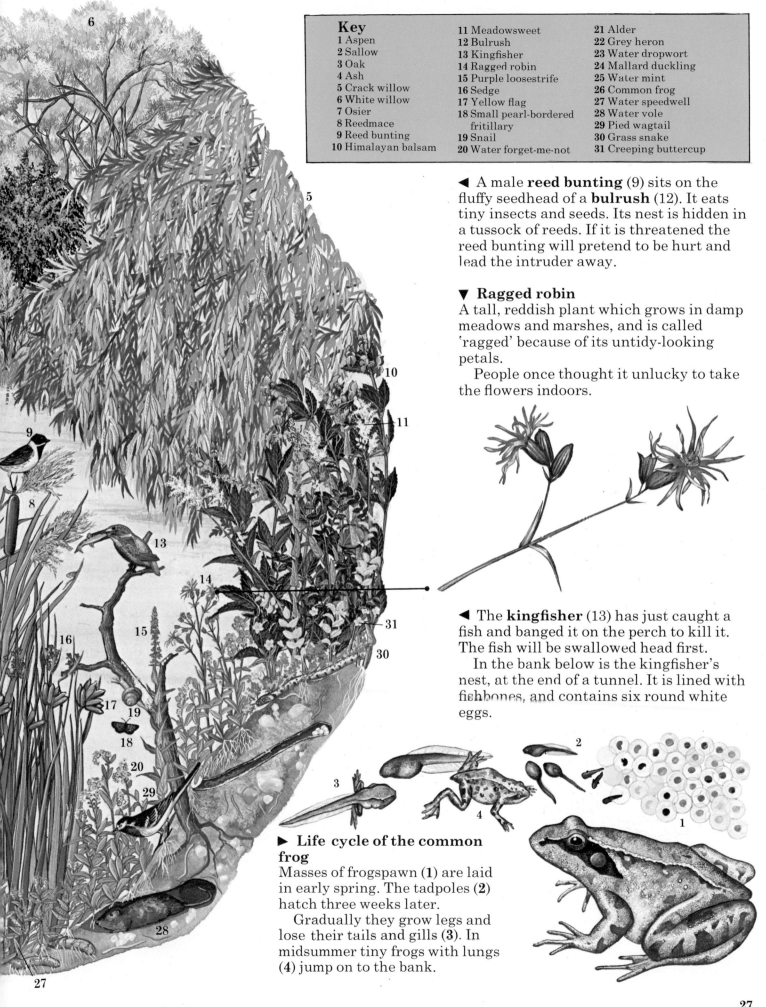

◀ A male **reed bunting** (9) sits on the fluffy seedhead of a **bulrush** (12). It eats tiny insects and seeds. Its nest is hidden in a tussock of reeds. If it is threatened the reed bunting will pretend to be hurt and lead the intruder away.

▼ **Ragged robin**
A tall, reddish plant which grows in damp meadows and marshes, and is called 'ragged' because of its untidy-looking petals.

People once thought it unlucky to take the flowers indoors.

◀ The **kingfisher** (13) has just caught a fish and banged it on the perch to kill it. The fish will be swallowed head first.

In the bank below is the kingfisher's nest, at the end of a tunnel. It is lined with fishbones, and contains six round white eggs.

▶ **Life cycle of the common frog**
Masses of frogspawn (1) are laid in early spring. The tadpoles (2) hatch three weeks later.

Gradually they grow legs and lose their tails and gills (3). In midsummer tiny frogs with lungs (4) jump on to the bank.

Plants on the bank

The soft, damp soil of the bank means that many different plants grow there.

Sedges and reeds often grow at the edge. Plants which grow further up the bank often have large leaves and brightly coloured flowers, like marsh marigolds.

*Not to scale. The height of upright plants is given.

▲ **White willow** 20m
This is one of the commonest willows. Its leaves are silvery-white underneath, so that the tree looks whitish when blown by the wind. In spring it has furry catkins, which grow before the leaves.

▲ **Meadowsweet** 150cm
A tall, leafy plant which often grows in clumps beside rivers and streams. In summer it has frothy clusters of tiny, sweet-scented flowers, each with five petals. It was once spread on floors to perfume rooms.

▲ **Great willowherb** 200cm
There are many willowherbs, and this is one of the largest. It grows on banks and has deep pink flowers in summer. These turn into long thin seedpods. When ripe they split, and the fluffy seeds are blown away.

▲ **Butterbur** 25cm
A low, spreading plant, found in damp meadows and near streams. The leaves can be up to 100cm wide. In late spring it has pink flowers which are clustered on a short, upright stem. Bees love this sweet-scented plant.

▲ **Purple loosestrife** 100–160cm
A tall, upright plant with a stiff hairy stem, and long narrow leaves. In summer it has tall spikes of bright rosy-purple flowers. It often grows in clumps on damp ground beside lakes, rivers and canals.

▲ **Balsam** 120cm
This is one of the balsams found on riverbanks. All of them have seedpods which explode when touched. Another name for this plant is Touch-me-not. Himalayan balsam has purple flowers and is taller.

▲ **Water speedwell** 15-45cm
A low, branching plant which grows at the edge of ponds and streams. In summer it has tall spikes of blue flowers. Each flower has four petals, which fall off easily when shaken by the wind or touched.

▲ **Water forget-me-not** 15-45cm
One of many species of forget-me-not. It grows in shady wet places, and spreads by sending out runners along the ground. These root where they touch earth.

Scattering seeds

Plants scatter their seeds so that the new plants will have room to grow.

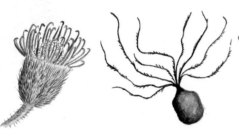

1 Agrimony 2 Willowherb 3 Cranesbill 4 Burdock

Agrimony (**1**) and burdock (**4**) have hooked seeds. They catch in animal fur and are carried away. Willowherb seeds (**2**) have hairy plumes, and float on the wind. The cranesbill fruit (**3**) explodes, shooting out the seeds.

▲ **Common reed** 300cm
A tall grass which grows at the edge of ponds, lakes and streams. It spreads by sending out underground stems. The stem and leaves are purplish-brown. In autumn it has clusters of tiny purplish-grey flowers.

▲ **Marsh marigold** 45cm
An early-flowering plant, seen on marshy ground and river banks in early spring. Clusters of yellow flowers contrast with the glossy green leaves, and then become round green seedpods. It is also called a kingcup.

▲ **Soft rush** 100-200cm
There are many kinds of rush. All are grass-like plants with long, narrow leaves, tall stems filled with pith, and greenish-brown flowers. Soft rush grows in damp meadows and near water, often forming tussocks.

▲ **Reedmace** 100–200cm
Often wrongly called a bulrush, the reedmace grows at the edge of ponds, lakes and streams, and is easily recognized by its tall brown seedhead. This bursts in spring, shedding the fluffy seeds to be blown away.

▲ **Branched bur-reed** 120cm
This sturdy plant grows near rivers and ponds. It has stiff, three-sided leaves and round flower-heads. The fruits are yellow-brown nuts which vary in shape. Some are round, others boat-shaped.

▲ **Common sedge** 200cm
There are many different sedges. All grow near water and in wet meadows. The stems are three-sided, and it has flat narrow, greyish leaves, which roll up when dry. The tiny greenish flowers grow in spikes.

▲ **Great pond sedge** 100–150cm
Usually found near ponds, lakes and slow-flowing streams or canals. It has thin green leaves. In autumn it grows a tall flower spike. The male flowers are clustered on a thin spike above the fatter female spike.

29

Autumn

Autumn is a time of slowing down. The days grow shorter and colder, and the sunlight gets weaker. Animals and plants are building up their strength for the cold, dark days ahead.

Plant life
Plants begin to die down. They stop flowering, but their seeds go on developing. The leaves often change colour as the plants stop making food through them.

▲ **The shiny yellow sulphur-tuft fungus grows in large clumps on tree stumps, like this alder. The gills turn dark brown when ripe.**

One sort of plant is mainly seen in autumn. Fungi live in the soil for most of the year. In autumn they produce fruiting bodies, such as mushrooms and toadstools. These release spores which may grow into new plants in the soil.

Tiny animals
As plants die or lose their leaves they rot in the damp weather. Many invertebrates, such as slugs and snails, eat rotting plants, so there are more of them to be seen in autumn. This is also the time of year when spiders migrate.

▲ **A female teal (left) landing near her colourful mate on a river. Some flocks breed in western Europe, while others arrive in late autumn.**

They have spent summer where they were hatched. Now thousands of tiny spiders climb to the top of twigs and launch themselves on the wind, each trailing a fine silk thread. They may be blown far away. Some will be eaten by birds, or land on the water and be snapped up by fishes and amphibians. Others will survive their flight and become adults far away from where they were hatched.

Most winged insects will die in the cold of winter. Their young survive, spending winter as pupae or nymphs, either underground or underwater.

As plants and insects die there is less food for animals. Instead of insects and leaves they eat pupae and seeds.

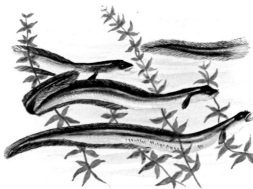

▲ **Eels migrating downstream towards the sea, where they will breed. Their colour has changed to silvery grey, and their heads are thinner.**

Seeds
Plants produce far more seeds than will grow. Some are eaten, some rot and some never reach a suitable place to grow. Plants shed their seeds in may different ways, trying to spread them as far as possible.

Underwater plants also die as the weather, and the water, grow colder. Some leave seeds or buds buried in the mud. These will grow into new plants.

Migration
Mature eels begin their long journey back to the sea where they were hatched. They have lived in fresh waters for ten to eighteen years.

▲ **An alder twig. By autumn the female flowers (bottom right) have become cones full of ripe seeds (top). On the left are young male catkins.**

Now the adults stop eating and swim towards the sea. There they cross the Atlantic to an area near Bermuda, where they breed and then die.

The eel larvae hatch and are carried back to European coastal waters. There they change into small eels, called elvers, and swim inland to live in rivers and streams.

Many birds fly south to warmer countries. They gather in great twittering flocks, then suddenly fly away.

Autumn fades into winter gradually as the days grow short, damp and cold.

Winter

In winter there seems to be very little activity near fresh waters. It is cold and dark, and food is hard to find. Often there is little water, because the ground is frozen.

Some animals come to ponds and streams to drink. Some come to find food – often other animals. There is also likely to be more plant life near running water than anywhere else, since plants need water.

▲ The cold winter wind strips seeds from fluffy reed heads. Many plants keep their seeds till winter. They provide food for hungry birds.

Hibernation

Animals have various ways of living through the winter. Many of them hibernate. This means that they go into a very deep sleep, so deep that they seem to be dead. They become cold, their heartbeat drops and they breathe very slowly. They live on fat which they have stored under the skin during the autumn. Most animals which hibernate are small and eat insects.

To avoid being eaten or dying of cold, animals usually hibernate in a sheltered place. Toads, lizards and snakes burrow under stones, earth or leaves.

▲ In very cold weather stretches of water may freeze over. The ice and snow act as insulating blankets, keeping the water below them warm.

Frogs and newts bury themselves in the mud at the bottom of ponds. Bats cluster together for warmth in sheltered places such as hollow trees.

Larger animals remain active throughout the winter. Mammals, such as otters and mink, grow thicker coats and store extra layers of fat during the autumn. Hunger often makes them bolder, and they may be seen hunting in daylight. By spring they will be thin and weak, and some will have died.

Water animals

Underwater life slows down, but is less affected by the cold, dark weather than life on the bank. Fish move more slowly, and some stop eating for the winter.

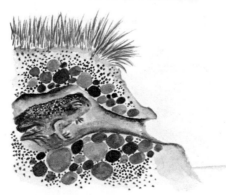

▲ A toad hibernates in a dry burrow above water-level. The ground helps to keep the toad warm, and hides it from hungry animals.

Invertebrates are still active. Even if the water is frozen over you may see diving beetles dashing about under the ice.

Birds

Flocks of coots gather on many lakes and reservoirs. They scare away intruders, such as a hungry fox, by splashing across the water, flapping their wings and raising clouds of spray.

Many birds come from further north. Siskins, small greenish finches, eat alder seeds.

Geese fly in from Russia and Greenland, honking as they pass overhead in V-shaped lines. Whooper and Bewick's swans also visit lakes and reservoirs.

▲ Many different geese fly south in winter. These are Canada geese, which have black necks and heads, with white cheek-patches.

Spring returns

As winter turns into spring the days get longer and warmer. Many plants and animals have died, but many more have survived.

Some plants spend the winter underground, as bulbs, corms and tubers. They are among the first to appear in spring, and include snowdrops and crocuses. Two other early flowering plants are coltsfoot and marsh marigold. These have yellow flowers, as do many spring plants.

The cycle of the year is complete, and spring begins again.

Animals that live near water

Many different animals live on the bank. As well as birds and invertebrates there are mammals, like otters, amphibians, like frogs, and reptiles, like snakes.

Mammals and reptiles breed on land but eat water plants or animals. Amphibians breed in water, but spend most of their lives on land.

*Not to scale. The size given is the body-length of a mature adult.

▲ **Muskrat** 26–40cm, tail 19–27cm
A large vole from North America, which lives in parts of Europe but not in Britain since 1937. It builds a lodge in shallow water and is a good swimmer and diver. It is nocturnal, and lives mainly on plants.

▲ **Water shrew** 76–96mm, tail 52–72mm
This tiny animal lives in a burrow near slow streams and in marshes. It swims and dives for short periods, and eats frogs, worms, insects and small fish. The owl is its chief enemy.

▲ **Coypu** 60cm
A large rodent, which is often mistaken for an otter. It escaped from fur farms in the 1930s. It eats plants and is active at night. Its burrowing can damage river banks and make them collapse.

▲ **Otter** 1.2m
A secretive, nocturnal mammal, which rests during the day in its holt, often a hole in a river bank. At night it hunts many different animals including frogs, fishes, moorhens, crayfish and water voles.

▲ **Water vole** 19–21cm, tail 11cm
Often confused with the brown rat, which also swims well. The water vole eats mainly bank plants. It lives in a burrow in the bank, and is very short-sighted. Many animals eat water voles.

▲ **Mink** 30-43cm, tail 13–23cm
This American relative of the weasel escaped from fur farms and now lives by many rivers, often in disused water vole burrows. It is nocturnal and swims well. Mink eat poultry as well as water animals.

Eggs, laid singly on water plants

Spawn

▲ **Fire-bellied toad** 4–5cm
This brightly-coloured amphibian is found in parts of Europe but not in Britain. It lives in streams and ponds. If any enemy threatens it the toad will stand on its hind legs and display its red-blotched underside.

▲ **Common toad** 6–10cm
Toads return to the water where they were hatched to breed. The female lays long strings of eggs which are twisted round water plants.
 At night toads hunt tiny animals such as worms.

▲ **Fire salamander** 30cm
Found in parts of Europe but not in Britain. It is a close relative of the newt, but gives birth to live young. They live in water for about four months, then spend the rest of their lives on land, in damp areas.

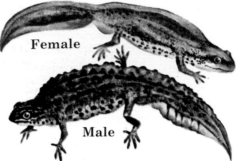

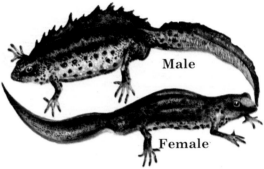

Female

Male

Male

Female

▲ **Grass snake** 60–100cm
Found throughout western Europe but not in Ireland, where there are no snakes. It lives near water and eats frogs, toads, newts and fish. In winter it hibernates in a hole. Young snakes hatch from eggs.

▲ **Smooth newt** 10cm
An amphibian, which lives mainly on land. At night it hunts for slugs, snails and insects. Its skin is dry and roughish. When it returns to water to breed, the male grows a crest and becomes more brightly coloured.

▲ **Great crested newt** 14–16cm
The largest European newt. It lives in fairly deep ponds and hibernates on land. In the breeding season the male grows a high ragged crest along his back and tail. When seized this newt gives out a nasty fluid.

▲ **Daubenton's bat** 8cm, wingspan 25cm
A small bat, also called the water bat. It can be seen flying before dusk, over streams, ponds and rivers, catching flying insects. It hibernates in hollow trees, hanging upside-down.

Animal footprints

You may see these in mud or snow. Hind foot (H) on left, fore foot (F) on right.

1 Otter H 4cm long, F 6cm   2 Mink H 4cm, F 3cm   3 Coypu H 12cm, F 6cm

4 Water vole H 3cm, F 2.5cm   5 Water shrew H 1.4cm, F 1.2 cm   6 Muskrat H 12cm, F 6cm

1 Web between toes may show, and claws may be tiny points.
2 Clear prints. Web may show.
3 Web may show on hind foot.
4 Star-shaped prints. Hind foot larger than fore.
5 Prints often faint, because shrews are very light.
6 Five toes on fore foot, but usually only four show.

A pond

Life in a pond is rich and varied. The water is still and warm. Plants grow easily in the muddy bottom, and give shelter to animals.

The plants and animals are linked in foodchains. All eat and all are eaten. This balance can be upset if the pond becomes polluted.

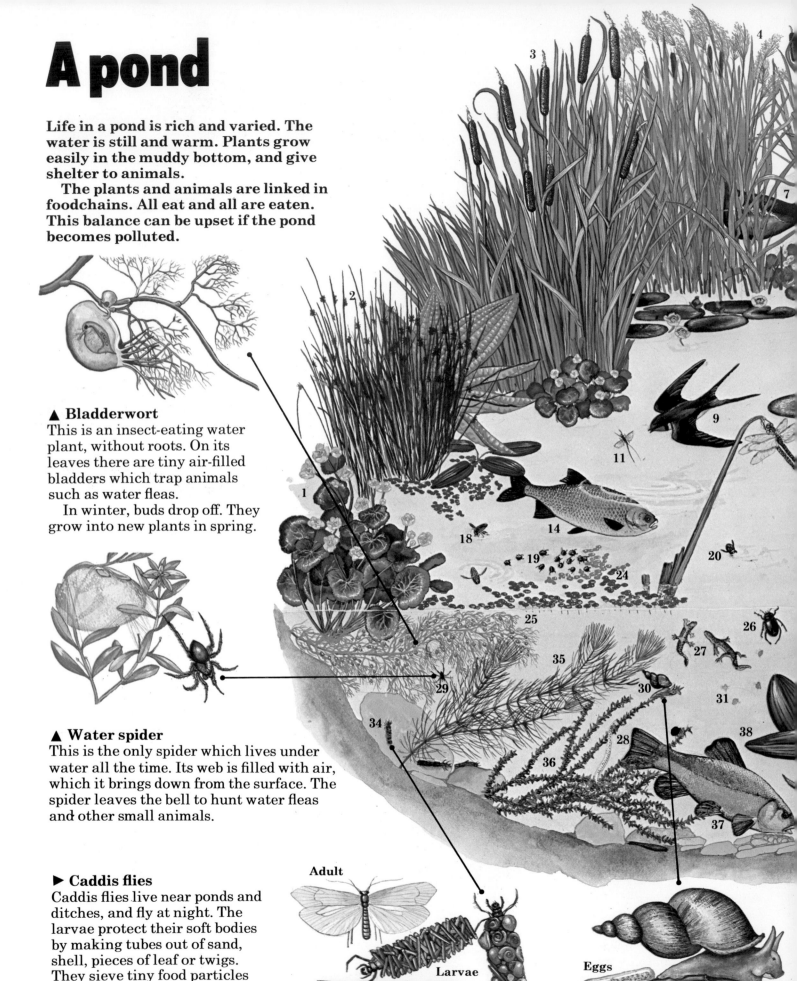

▲ Bladderwort

This is an insect-eating water plant, without roots. On its leaves there are tiny air-filled bladders which trap animals such as water fleas.

In winter, buds drop off. They grow into new plants in spring.

▲ Water spider

This is the only spider which lives under water all the time. Its web is filled with air, which it brings down from the surface. The spider leaves the bell to hunt water fleas and other small animals.

▶ Caddis flies

Caddis flies live near ponds and ditches, and fly at night. The larvae protect their soft bodies by making tubes out of sand, shell, pieces of leaf or twigs. They sieve tiny food particles from the water.

Adult

Larvae

Eggs

34

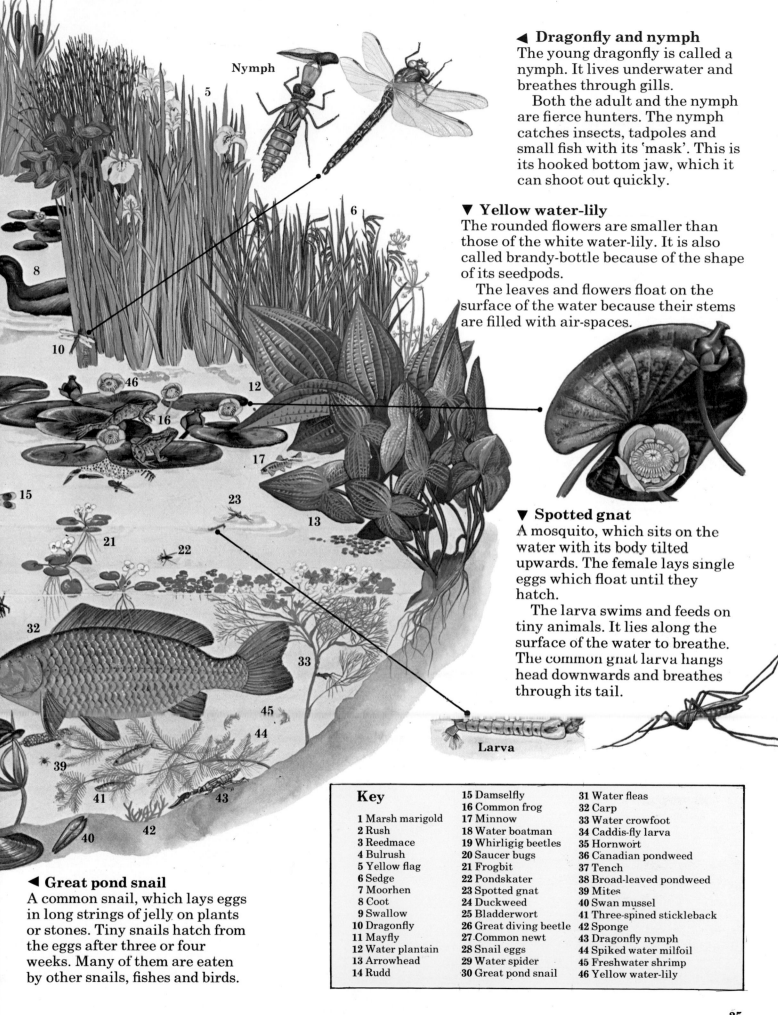

Nymph

5

8

10

46

16

12

17

13

15

23

21

22

32

33

45

44

39

41

43

42

40

6

◀ Dragonfly and nymph

The young dragonfly is called a nymph. It lives underwater and breathes through gills.

Both the adult and the nymph are fierce hunters. The nymph catches insects, tadpoles and small fish with its 'mask'. This is its hooked bottom jaw, which it can shoot out quickly.

▼ Yellow water-lily

The rounded flowers are smaller than those of the white water-lily. It is also called brandy-bottle because of the shape of its seedpods.

The leaves and flowers float on the surface of the water because their stems are filled with air-spaces.

▼ Spotted gnat

A mosquito, which sits on the water with its body tilted upwards. The female lays single eggs which float until they hatch.

The larva swims and feeds on tiny animals. It lies along the surface of the water to breathe. The common gnat larva hangs head downwards and breathes through its tail.

Larva

◀ Great pond snail

A common snail, which lays eggs in long strings of jelly on plants or stones. Tiny snails hatch from the eggs after three or four weeks. Many of them are eaten by other snails, fishes and birds.

Key		
	15 Damselfly	31 Water fleas
	16 Common frog	32 Carp
1 Marsh marigold	17 Minnow	33 Water crowfoot
2 Rush	18 Water boatman	34 Caddis-fly larva
3 Reedmace	19 Whirligig beetles	35 Hornwort
4 Bulrush	20 Saucer bugs	36 Canadian pondweed
5 Yellow flag	21 Frogbit	37 Tench
6 Sedge	22 Pondskater	38 Broad-leaved pondweed
7 Moorhen	23 Spotted gnat	39 Mites
8 Coot	24 Duckweed	40 Swan mussel
9 Swallow	25 Bladderwort	41 Three-spined stickleback
10 Dragonfly	26 Great diving beetle	42 Sponge
11 Mayfly	27 Common newt	43 Dragonfly nymph
12 Water plantain	28 Snail eggs	44 Spiked water milfoil
13 Arrowhead	29 Water spider	45 Freshwater shrimp
14 Rudd	30 Great pond snail	46 Yellow water-lily

Tiny animals in the water

Some water invertebrates, like pondskaters, live on top of the water. Some, like snails, live under the water but have to return to the surface for air. They live in shallow water. Some, like leeches, use dissolved oxygen, and live in deeper water.

*Not to scale. The size given is the body-length of a mature adult.

▲ **Water scorpion** 1–2cm
The long 'tail' is a breathing tube, not a sting. This bug lives in shallow weedy water, and is a bad swimmer. It catches insects, tadpoles and small fishes with its front legs, and sucks out their juices with its beak.

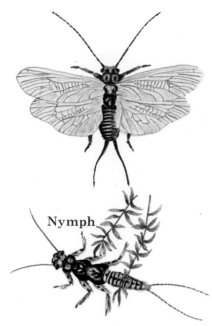

Nymph

▲ **Stonefly** 6–12mm
The nymphs live underwater for up to three years, but the adults live for only two to three weeks. They have two pairs of wings, which are folded flat when resting. Although they can fly, they are usually seen hiding under stones near fast-flowing water.

▲ **Water stick insect** 30–35mm
Like the water scorpion, this bug has a long breathing tube and lives near the edges of still water. Its eggs also have breathing tubes.

▲ **Pondskater** 14–17mm
This long-legged bug skims over the surface of ponds and lakes. It rows with its middle legs and steers with its hind legs, held up by the surface tension. It sucks the juices from small insects such as water fleas.

Female

Male

▲ **Water measurer** 8–12mm
This bug walks slowly on the surface of still water in ponds and ditches. It stabs tiny animals, such as water fleas, with its sharp beak. In winter it rests under a stone on land.

▲ **Backswimmer** 15mm
This lively bug swims on its back, using its fringed legs to propel it through the water. It hunts tadpoles and beetle larvae. Air from the surface is trapped in the hairs covering its body, making it look silver.

▲ **Great diving beetle** 35mm
A fierce hunter, found in ponds. It breathes by floating to the surface tail first and letting air flow under its wingcases. The larvae have huge pincers and will attack anything from other beetles to small fishes.

▲ Whirligig beetle 5–6mm
A tiny black beetle, often seen in groups. It swims in circles on the surface of ponds with its back out of the water. It can dive underwater, carrying an air bubble. Its larvae live on the bottom, and have gills.

Breathing underwater

These are four different ways of taking in oxygen from the surface.

1 Great diving beetle
2 Great silver beetle
3 Common gnat larva
4 Water spider

The great diving beetle (1) takes in air at its hind end. The great silver beetle (2) breaks the surface with one of its antennae. Both store the air under their wingcases. The gnat larva (3) breathes through a tube. The water spider (4) stores air in its underwater web.

▲ Great silver beetle 40mm
This beetle eats mainly plants. To breathe it rises to the surface and breaks the surface tension with one of its antennae, so that air can flow under its wingcases. The trapped air makes it look silver when it dives.

▲ Great pond snail 5–6cm
Very common in ponds and weedy lakes. It feeds on algae and dead animals. Its eggs are laid in a jelly capsule holding up to 300 eggs. Each hatches into a tiny snail. An adult can have up to eight whorls on its tall shell.

▲ Great ramshorn snail 35mm wide
Unlike other snails the ramshorn has red blood. It lives in ponds, weedy lakes and slow-flowing rivers, eating algae and decaying plants and animals. Its shell is flattened, with five or six whorls.

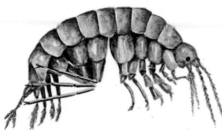

▲ Freshwater shrimp 20mm
Found in large numbers under stones and among plants in most clean streams, ponds and shallow lakes. It swims on its side, and you will often find a female carrying a smaller male. It eats mainly decaying plants, and is eaten by many fishes. The female lays eggs in brood pouches on her legs.

▲ Horse leech 15cm
Found in ponds and slow-flowing water. Some leeches suck blood but this one swallows small animals such as worms and insect larvae whole. It has a sucking disc at each end of its body.

▲ Tubifex worms 3cm
Colonies of these bright red worms live on the muddy bottoms of slow-flowing streams and rivers. Their waving 'tails' make a current, which brings fresh oxygen to them. If disturbed they draw back into their tubes.

Pollution

What happens to waste?

All animals and plants die. This is part of the natural cycle of life. When they die, their remains sink to the bottom of the water, where tiny organisms, called bacteria, break them down. They become part of the material on the bottom and in the water, which other plants and animals feed on.

Bacteria need oxygen to break down dead plants and animals. If there is too much dead matter all the oxygen will be used up before the bacteria have broken down all the waste. The water will seem to be dead.

However, some bacteria do not need oxygen, and slowly they break down the extra waste. The water becomes clean again.

Chemical pollution

Bacteria cannot clean water which has been polluted by chemicals. The balance of the water is altered.

Some chemicals are poisonous to fish, and kill them directly. The waste which many factories pour into the water often contains poisonous chemicals. Insecticides, sprayed on to crops and then blown into nearby waters, also poison fish.

▼ **How water is polluted**
Rivers are fresh and clean when they start, but may be lifeless by the time they reach the sea.

Pollution is caused by people. These are just five of the ways in which the balance of freshwater life is upset.

▼ **Many farmers spray their fields with chemical fertilizers. The rain washes these into nearby rivers and streams, where they upset the chemical balance of the water. Plants grow too fast and block out the light.**

▼ **The village pond is often used as a rubbish dump. People throw in anything from household waste to old cars, thinking the water will hide everything. The results look terrible, and destroy the life of the pond.**

Other chemicals have an indirect effect. They alter the balance of the water so that plants grow too fast and block out the light. A layer of algae covers the surface, so that no oxygen or light can enter the water. Underwater plants die. There is nothing for small animals, such as insect larvae and water fleas, to eat, so they die. Without food or oxygen larger animals die. The water becomes empty and dead, with an unpleasant smell and scum covering the surface.

This sort of pollution can be caused by chemical fertilizers from fields, or by waste being dumped. Waste may also make the water cloudy, so that plants cannot get light. They die, and so do the animals which eat them.

Destroying habitats
Another form of water pollution is the destruction of the places where plants and animals live – their habitats. Rivers, lakes and reservoirs are often used for water-skiing and pleasure-cruising. The wash from motorboats breaks down the banks, and their engines leave an oily film on the water, blocking out oxygen and light.

What you can do
You can help to stop habitats being destroyed. Think about the animals and plants you see. They have a right to live too. Don't pick wild flowers or dig them up. If you're having a picnic, take your rubbish home or put it in a litter-bin. Though these may seem to be small things, they are very important.

It is easy to destroy a habitat, and impossible to replace it. By destroying the balance of life in fresh waters we are destroying ourselves, for we depend on animals and plants for our food and oxygen.

▼ **Factories are often built beside rivers. They use the water in their manufacturing processes and pour poisonous chemical wastes back into the river. These kill freshwater life, and make the river look and smell foul.**

▼ **Power stations use water in their cooling towers and then return it to the river, when it is warmer than the river water. This makes plants grow too fast. Fish may be killed by the rise in temperature.**

▼ **Sewage works also use water, running it through sewage to help break it down. This process takes large amounts of oxygen from the water, so that animals cannot live there. It also fills the water with black sludge.**

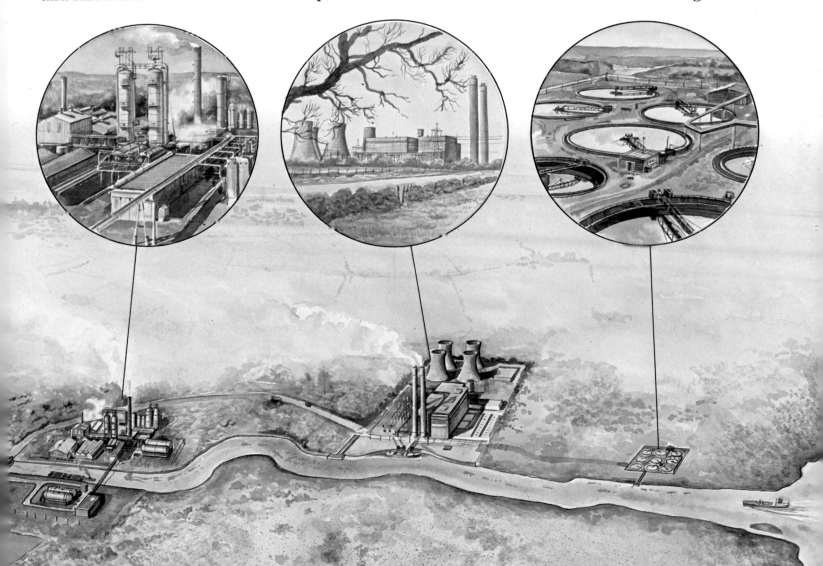

Lakes and canals

Still or running water?
Freshwater habitats are either still water or running water. A pond is still water. There is no current, so the water stays in the same place. A river is running water. There is a current, caused by the movement of the water downhill towards the sea. Some plants and animals are suited to living in still water, others prefer running water.

Lakes
Lakes are still-water habitats. They are colder than ponds, because the water is deeper. The sun warms the water near the edge and at the surface, so you will find many pond plants and animals in these areas.

Because lakes are larger and colder than ponds, river plants and animals also live there. You may find many different fishes including trout, perch, eels, pike and miller's thumbs.

▲ **Lock gates on a canal. Canals are artificial rivers. They run slowly, and are like long thin ponds.**

In the reeds at the edge warblers look for insects, and mallard, moorhens and teal build their nests. Herons stalk frogs and fish in the shallows. Over deeper parts of the lake you may see diving birds, such as coots, grebes, tufted ducks, pochard and mergansers.

In the deeper parts of a lake the water is always cold. Tiny animals called plankton live here.

Artificial lakes
A reservoir is like a lake, but has been made to hold water, usually behind a dam. Sometimes a dam is built across the end of a valley in which there is a river, and the whole valley is flooded.

▲ **This is a gravel-pit, which has been flooded. Trees have been planted, and it is now a deep artificial lake.**

Another kind of artificial lake is made by flooding old quarries. Huge holes are left in the ground where gravel and chalk have been dug out, and these make deep lakes with steeply-sloping sides. They are often used for sports like water-skiing or powerboat racing.

Canals
Canals are running-water habitats, like streams and rivers. They were dug to carry goods between towns.

Most of a canal's water comes from nearby rivers and streams. The water only flows quickly when the lock gates are opened.

▲ **Old streams are often choked with weed. They are favourite spawning grounds for frogs, toads and newts.**

This means that a canal is like a shallow lake or pond, and has many still-water plants and animals. But because it is connected to a river you will also find some plants and animals which live in running water. Many stretches of canal are no longer used. They are cut off from rivers, and contain only still-water life.

Life in canals
The edges of a canal are thick with plants and water weeds, but the middle is kept clear by boats. Small animals, such as water fleas, dragonfly nymphs, caddis-fly larvae and water boatmen, live near the edges. Near locks, where the water is often stirred up, freshwater sponges and mosses grow thickly on the walls. Water voles dig burrows in the banks of the canal, and eat water snails and freshwater mussels from the bottom.

The flowers of curled pondweed and spiked water milfoil float on the surface. Reedmace, yellow flag and common reed often grow along the towpath. They make good nesting sites for many birds.

Dabchicks, or little grebes, make their nests in the floating plants at the water's edge. During the day swallows and swifts fly low over the water, snatching insects from the air. At night you may see bats.

Looking at water-life

Look for freshwater life in streams, ditches, lakes, rivers, reservoirs, canals and ponds, no matter how small. You will see most in spring and summer.

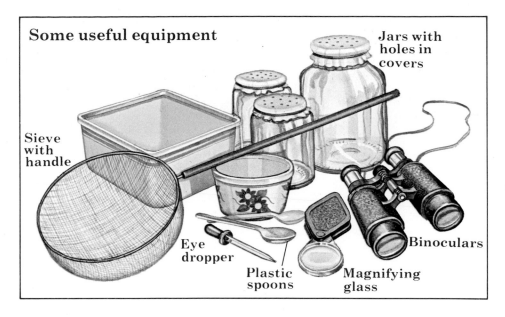

Some useful equipment

Jars with holes in covers

Sieve with handle

Eye dropper

Plastic spoons

Magnifying glass

Binoculars

Dos and don'ts
1. Always move slowly and quietly.
2. Test the depth of the water before walking in.
3. Replace stones and logs as they were.
4. Study specimens by the water if possible. If you want to take them home, put them in plastic jars and keep them cool in the shade.
Don't take more specimens than necessary, and **don't** take whole plants.
5. **Don't** take large animals such as frogs home. They are very difficult to keep alive.
6. Return all your specimens to the place where you found them *as soon as possible.*

Making an aquarium
If you want to look at specimens at home, you should keep them in an aquarium so that they have enough space and air.

Cover the bottom with mud from the place where you found your specimens. Water plants will root in this.

Fill the aquarium with pond water if you can. If not, use tap water and leave it to stand for a few days first. Mix some pond water with it. Let the water clear before you put your specimens in.

What to take
The best equipment for studying freshwater life is a notebook and a pencil. With these you can make notes, sketches and observations.

The simple equipment shown above will also help you.

How to use equipment
Collect tiny animals with an *eye-dropper*, and larger ones with a *sieve*. Pick up animals with a *plastic spoon* so that you don't squash them. Put them in *clean plastic jars*, and study them through a *magnifying glass*.

A freshwater aquarium

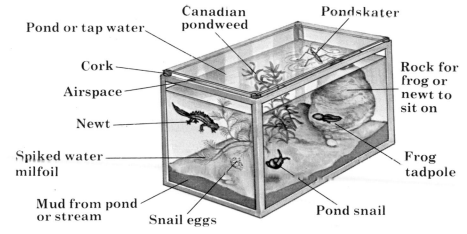

Pond or tap water

Canadian pondweed

Pondskater

Cork

Airspace

Newt

Spiked water milfoil

Mud from pond or stream

Snail eggs

Rock for frog or newt to sit on

Frog tadpole

Pond snail

If you have a tadpole or newt in your aquarium, put a flat-topped rock at one end, sticking out of the water. When the tadpole turns into an adult it will drown if it cannot leave the water. Newts also breathe air.

Cover your aquarium with a sheet of glass or heavy plastic, resting on a cork at each corner so that air can get in.

What to keep
A snail will keep the glass clean by eating the algae which grow there. It will probably lay eggs, which you can watch as they hatch into tiny snails.

Keep fierce animals, such as great diving beetles, water scorpions and water boatmen, on their own. They will eat all your other animals!

Word list

Amphibian Vertebrate which lives on land but breeds in water. Its young are larvae or tadpoles. They live in water and have gills. Frogs, toads, newts and salamanders are amphibians.

Aquatic Living in water.

Brood The young from a single clutch of eggs. Used of birds.

Carnivores Animals or plants that eat animals.

Crustaceans Invertebrates which live mainly in water and have a hard shell, breathe through gills and have two pairs of antennae. Freshwater shrimps, crayfish and water fleas are all crustaceans.

Deciduous A tree which loses its leaves in winter.

Diurnal Active by day.

Dormant Resting. Many plants pass the winter in a dormant state.

Eclipse plumage Dull colouring of male ducks for a period after the breeding season.

Erosion The wearing away of rocks and soil by water.

Evergreen A tree which does not lose its leaves in winter.

Habitat The natural surroundings of a plant or animal.

Herbivores Animals that eat plants.

Hibernation Passing the winter in a deep sleep.

Incubation Sitting on eggs until they hatch. Used of birds.

Insectivores Birds or mammals that feed mainly on insects. For example, shrews are insectivores.

Invertebrate Animal without a backbone. Insects, spiders, crustaceans and molluscs are all invertebrates.

Larva The young stage of many animals. Tadpoles are the larvae of frogs and toads. In insects, this is the stage between leaving the egg and becoming a pupa. Caterpillars are the larvae of butterflies and moths.

Mammals Animals which have a backbone and breathe air. The young are usually born alive and then feed on their mother's milk. Otters and coypu are both mammals.

Metamorphosis Change of shape in insect life history e.g. egg to larva to pupa to adult or egg to nymph to adult.

Migration The movement of animals, usually with the change in seasons. Many birds migrate south in winter.

Mollusc Animal with a muscular 'foot' and, usually, a hard shell. Snails, slugs and freshwater mussels are all molluscs.

Nocturnal Active at night.

Nymph Stage of insect development between egg and adult. A nymph looks like an adult but has no wings. Insects which have nymphs do not go through a pupal stage. Dragonflies and mayflies are insects which have nymphs.

Parasite An animal or plant which feeds on another animal or plant, called the host, without killing it.

Predator An animal which kills other animals for food.

Pupa Stage in insect development between larva and adult. The pupa, which usually has a hard covering, does not feed and is almost motionless. However during this time adult features, such as wings and legs, are formed. Caddis flies and butterflies are insects which have pupae.

Resident An animal which lives in one country or region throughout the year.

Vertebrate Animal with a backbone. Fishes, amphibians, reptiles, birds and mammals are all vertebrates.

How to find out more

Clubs

One way of finding out more is to join a club. There are several different ones with junior sections, which will help you learn more about freshwater habitats. They organize outings and have regular meetings at which you can talk to people who have similar interests. Some societies have their own nature reserves, where you can see rare animals and plants in protected habitats.

Always enclose a stamped addressed envelope when you write for information.

You can get the addresses of your local **Natural History Society** and local **County Naturalist Trust** from
Council for Nature
The Zoological Society
Regent's Park
London NW1 4RY

The **British Naturalists' Association** has a quarterly magazine with a special section for junior members. For more information write to
Mrs Y. Griffiths
23 Oak Hill Close
Woodford Green
Essex 1G8 9PH

The **Royal Society for the Protection of Birds (RSPB)** has a junior branch, the **Young Ornithologists' Club (YOC)**. You can belong to this if you are under 15. It arranges outings and meetings, and produces a magazine called *Bird Life*. This contains articles by experts and members, information on competitions and projects, and club news. Members also receive a membership card and badge. For more information and an enrolment form write to
YOC
The Lodge
Sandy
Bedfordshire

The **Watch Club** is run by the *Sunday Times* and the **County Nature Conservation Trust**. It is for 10 to 15 year-olds and organizes projects and other activities. One recent activity was to invent an easy way of measuring water pollution. Membership is very cheap, and members receive the magazine, *Watchword,* three times a year. For more information write to
Watch
22 The Green
Nettleham
Lincoln LN2 2NR

Books

There are hundreds of books about European wildlife. Those listed here are only a very small selection. Visit your local **bookshops** and **libraries** to find what else is available.

If you are not already a member of the local library, it would be an excellent idea for you to join.

These books will all give you more information on some aspects of **freshwater wildlife**:
The Ecology of Waterlife Alfred Leutscher (Franklin Watts). Good informative book about life in rivers, ponds, marshes and the sea.
Pond and Marsh James Whinray (A & C Black). Quite useful introduction to these habitats.
Pond and Stream Life edited by John Clegg (Blandford Press). A useful identification guide to invertebrates and amphibians living in fresh waters.
Pond Life Ralph Whitlock (Wayland). Good introductory book.
The Pond Book John Dyson (Penguin). All about ponds; how to study them, their importance, how to stop them being polluted.
Ponds and Streams Su Swallow (Usborne Nature-trail series). Fun to read, suggests activities.
The Natural History of Britain and Northern Europe: Rivers, Lakes and Marshes (Hodder & Stoughton). A good reference book with an informative introductory essay on freshwater habitats.
Rivers and Lakes Keith Lye (Macdonald New Reference Library). A very good introduction to these habitats.

Identification
There are several series of good identification guides.
The *Observer's Book of . . .* series includes guides to Wild flowers, Trees, Birds, Butterflies, Freshwater fishes, Common insects and spiders, and Pond life.
The *Oxford Book of . . .* series includes guides to Vertebrates, Invertebrates, Insects, Birds, Wild flowers, and Flowerless plants. They are large and very informative. The guide to Vertebrates includes fishes, amphibians and mammals.
The *Usborne Spotter's Guide to . . .* series includes guides to Birds, Fishes, Wild flowers, Trees, Animals, Tracks and Signs, and Insects. They are small and cheap.

The **Natural History Museum** produces very good identification **wallcharts** on Mammals, Fishes, Birds, Trees, Flowers and Insects. They are available from
Publications Department
British Museum (Natural History)
Cromwell Road
London SW7

Fishes
Freshwater Fishing Brian Ward (Macdonald Guidelines). Has a good section on identification of fishes.
Freshwater Fishes of Britain and Europe B.J. Muus (Collins). The standard reference book.

Birds
Birds John Andrews (Hamlyn Nature Guide). Good photographs.
The RSPB Guide to British Birds D. Saunders (Hamlyn). Good illustrations.
A Field Guide to the Birds of Britain and Europe R.T. Peterson, G. Mountford and P.A.D. Hollom (Collins). A standard reference book.
The Birdlife of Britain Philip Burton and Peter Hayman (Mitchell Beazley/RSPB).
Birds of Lake, River, Marsh and Field Lars Johnson (Penguin).
Birdwatcher's Pocket Guide (Mitchell Beazley). Very useful, small, well illustrated.
Birds of Britain and Europe Bertel Bruun (Hamlyn). Very good reference book.
Birds Christopher Perrins (Collins Countryside series). An informative book about the life of birds.
Bird Count Humphrey Dobinson (hardback Kestrel, paperback Peacock). How to study birds.
Birds Neil Ardley (Macdonald New Reference Library). A good introduction to bird life.

Mammals
Guide to the Mammals of Britain and Europe Maurice Burton (Elsevier/Phaidon). Useful divisions into habitats. Well illustrated.

Insects
A Field Guide to the Insects of Britain and Northern Europe Michael Chinery (Collins). Very good reference book.
Insects in Colour edited by N.D. Riley (Blandford Press). Small, informative.
Insects Matthew Prior (A & C Black).
Insects Mary and Paul Whalley (Macdonald New Reference Library). Very interesting introduction to the world of insects.

Flowers
The Concise British Flora in Colour W. Keble Martin (Ebury Press/Michael Joseph). Large, good illustrations.
Wild Flowers of Britain Roger Phillips (Pan). Very good photographs.
The Wild Flowers of Britain and Northern Europe R. Fitter, A. Fitter and M. Blamey (Collins). A good, cheap, reference book.
Wild Flowers Helen L. Pursey (Hamlyn Nature Guide). Good photographs.

General
Nature through the Seasons Richard Adams and M. Hooper (Penguin). Looks at various habitats. Lovely illustrations, informative.
The Countryside in Spring/Summer/Autumn/Winter (Jarrold). Good colour photographs, showing various habitats in each season.
Nature at Work (British Museum (Natural History)/CUP). A very good introduction to ecology. Well illustrated.

Index